A MOTHER'S HEART

Dale Jenkins
Jeff A. Jenkins

THIS BOOK IS PRESENTED TO:

_____

BY:

_____

ON THE DATE OF:

_____

DEDICATION

We dedicate this book to our mother, the woman who stood beside and behind our dad. Mamie Frame Jenkins was a delight to be around, a humble, faithful spouse and Christian who is probably the primary force behind our determining to preach. And to the mom's of our children, Laura and Melanie who dedicated their lives to helping our children find Jesus but still can't find socks.

A NOTE FROM THE AUTHORS

Mom and Moms:

Our mom was a unique lady. She lived in the shadow of a man she idolized and taught us to respect and revere. She was the last of 13 children and grew up in poverty, picking cotton but she never complained about it. She had a beautiful singing voice and loved to sing with her family. Like most moms she did not mind embarrassing us and she was always our greatest fan. In her eyes her children could do no wrong. Dad was a "superstar" to many - but it was mom who stood behind and beside him. She was the one who went to ballgames, worked two jobs, counseled, convicted, and taught us. She was the one who would say, "Your dad is off doing the greatest work in the world." She could have complained that dad was never home but she encouraged us that what he was doing was significant. Mom was stern and fun. She was old school in her theology but practical in her grace. She was humble and God lifts up the humble…so do we in this effort to honor mom's everywhere.

-Dale & Jeff

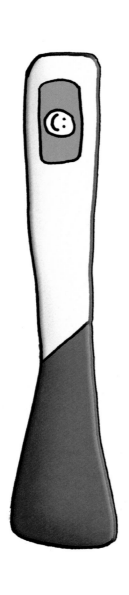

One day you
will wonder,
"Could I be
expecting?"

And when
you learn
you ARE:
**Your life is
never the
same.**

You will become a
PARENT...

... a MOTHER...

... a mom...

"mom."

Separated only by a push
and a cry you
will experience a pain
beyond description
and a love greater than
life.

**All the pain will go
away when you get to
hold your baby.**

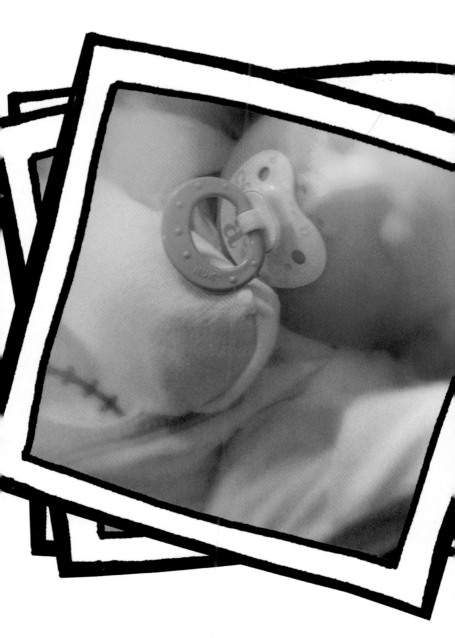

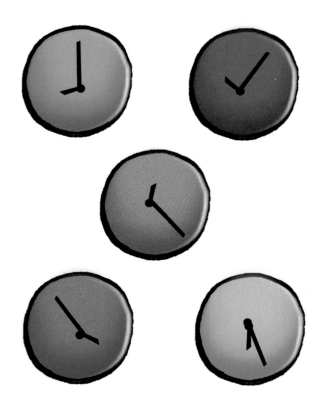

You will experience
sleepless nights on end
from the moment your
child is born.

You will pray like <u>never</u> before.

Even though you gave birth to, sat up with, changed, fed, and clothed her, she will say "daddy" first. But you will hear the word "mama" for the first time from your child and you'll forget *all* of that.

You will be taken for granted most of the time but will be honored with "elaborately" designed child made gifts that are the best they have to offer.

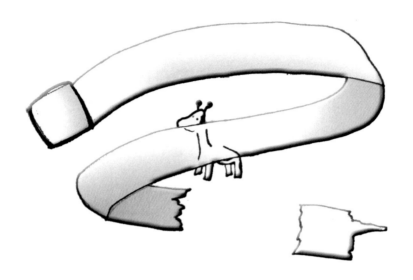

You will fight a never ending battle against your child's ability to make a mess.

You will be undervalued,
underpaid, and under
appreciated but a hug
and a few minutes
rocking your baby will
make it all better.

When your children are
small the days are long
but the years fly by.

You will pick up the same toy ten times in a day.

You will say the word
"no" 1,000 times
each day.

You will wonder where
the time went.

You will officiate over more fights than most ringmasters.

You will kiss a million boo-boo's.

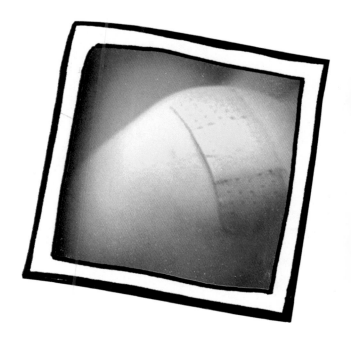

You will prepare
thousands of meals.

You will have dirty
laundry that seems to
multiply
and you're not sure if
you'll ever catch up.

The next day you will
start all over again.

You will deal with the
product that comes out
of any orifice of the
human body.

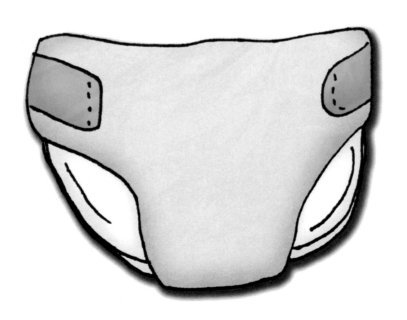

"That" favorite shirt...
the one you washed 500
times... the one you had
to fight him just to get it
off... You'll never want to
throw it away- for it
holds memories and is
now *your* favorite shirt.

You will carpool to ball games, band practices, and sleep overs and log more miles than most Yellow Cab drivers.

You will plan birthday
parties that would make
the royal family jealous.

You will rush
every Sunday trying to
get the family out the
door to church ONLY to
deal with a major
"blowout" in the car on
the way there.

You will cry a ton of tears as you send your child out on the first day of school.

Your child will think you are foolish... until they have their own child.

You will embarrass your son when you kiss him in public...

Secretly he will be happy in the security and knowledge of your love.

You will discover your
keys in the oddest of
places.

You might even lock
them in the car...with
your child inside.

You will wonder
why.

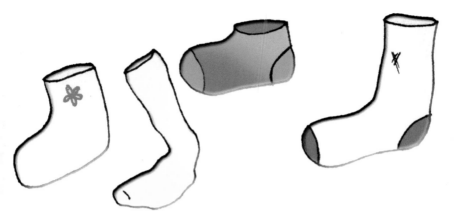

You will lose a gazillion
socks.

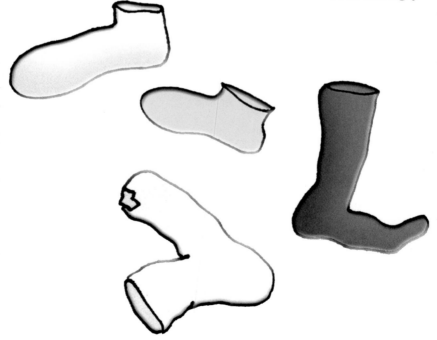

You will take your
daughter shopping for
clothes, and you will
spend hours looking.

(You will question
the meaning of "seek
and ye shall find").

When your child is sick, hurting, sad, or mistreated you will leap tall buildings to make it right.

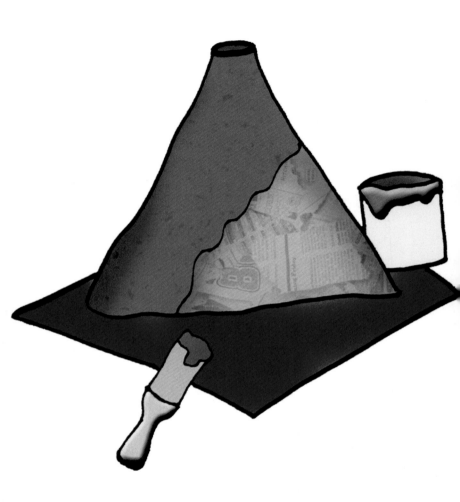

You will oversee more science fair projects than Thomas Edison.

You will try to sell more
Girl Scout cookies than
those little cookie elves
can make...

You'll end up buying
most of them yourself.

You will be the dispenser
of bandaids, Kool-aid,
and wisdom.

You will spend hours getting every hair in place for the annual family Christmas picture - it'll rain that day.

...Where *are* those socks?

You will receive
homemade Mother's
Day gifts that you will
cherish forever.

You will work on a thousand math problems.

You will learn to speak in text...

Lol

(INTERJECTION)
"LAUGH OUT LOUD"

(SALUTATION)
"TALK TO YOU LATER"

TTYL

IMO

(PREFACE)
"IN MY OPINION"

(EXPRESSION)
"I DON'T SPEAK 'TEXT'"

HUH?!?

Read 9:44 PM

You will make enough trips to the emergency room that you believe they should name a wing of it in your honor.

You will weep a million tears but laugh a billion laughs.

You will tell your children one million times not to exaggerate.

You'll see her pretending to be you talking on the cell phone and then you won't find it for hours.

The sock monster will haunt your dreams.

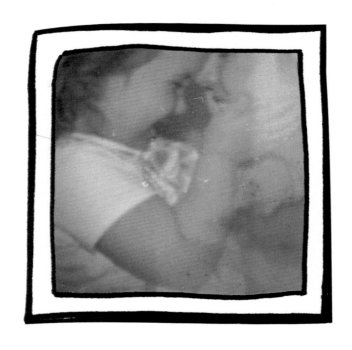

Your child will believe your voice is the most beautiful sound in the universe.

It won't matter how big he gets or how fancy his title—he will delight in kissing his mom in public.

Your children will rise up and call you blessed... and your husband too.

PROVERBS 31

A wife of noble character who can find?
She is worth far more than rubies.
Her husband has full confidence in her
and lacks nothing of value.
She brings him good, not harm,
all the days of her life.
She selects wool and flax
and works with eager hands.
She is like the merchant ships,
bringing her food from afar.
She gets up while it is still night;
she provides food for her family
and portions for her female servants.
She considers a field and buys it;
out of her earnings she plants a vineyard.
She sets about her work vigorously;
her arms are strong for her tasks.
She sees that her trading is profitable,
and her lamp does not go out at night.

In her hand she holds the distaff
and grasps the spindle with her fingers.
She opens her arms to the poor
and extends her hands to the needy.
When it snows, she has no fear for her
household;
for all of them are clothed in scarlet.
She makes coverings for her bed;
she is clothed in fine linen and purple.
Her husband is respected at the city gate,
where he takes his seat among the elders of
the land.
She makes linen garments and sells them,
and supplies the merchants with sashes.
She is clothed with strength and dignity;
she can laugh at the days to come.
She speaks with wisdom,
and faithful instruction is on her tongue.
She watches over the affairs of her household
and does not eat the bread of idleness.
Her children arise and call her blessed;
her husband also, and he praises her:
"Many women do noble things,
but you surpass them all."
Charm is deceptive, and beauty is fleeting;
but a woman who fears the Lord is to be
praised.
Honor her for all that her hands have done,
and let her works bring her praise at the city
gate.

Your child will see
Jesus through you
**and you will be her
hero.**

...Jesus didn't need
socks anyway.

Made in the USA
Columbia, SC
02 May 2019